GW00374378

The Cat NOT in the Hat!

A PARODY

By Dr. Juice

AS TOLD TO ALAN KATZ
ILLUSTRATED BY CHRIS WRINN

DOVE
BOOKS

BRENTWOOD, USA...

The other way.

A happy town
Inside L.A.
Where rich folks play
The day away.

But under the moon
The 12th of June.
Two victims flail
Assault! Assail!
Somebody will go to jail!
Who will it be?
Oh my! Oh me!

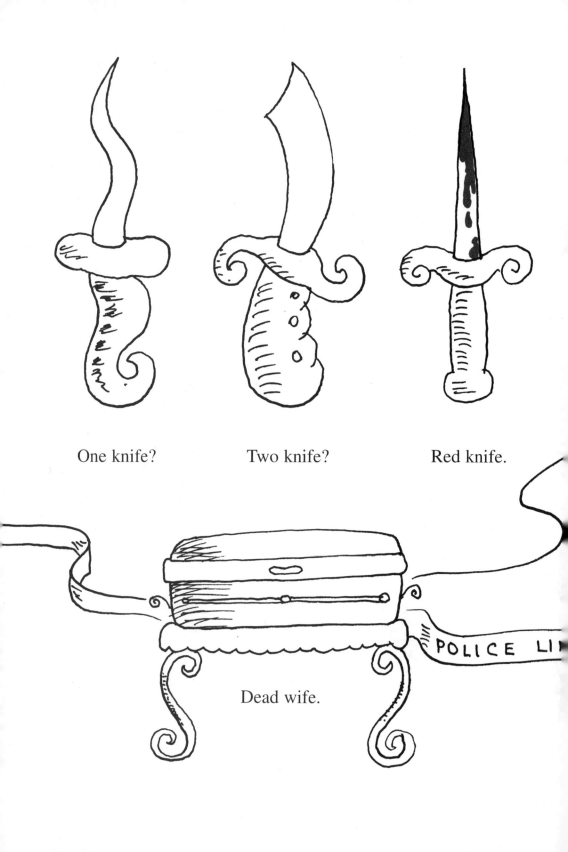

One knife?   Two knife?   Red knife.

Dead wife.

POLICE LI

Not far away.
There lived O.J.
A football hero-actor.
Yeah!

That night at McD's...the cash was Kato's
Juice had a shake and large french fried potatoes
Then wolfed down his burger behind the wheel
Say, what a quick and happy meal!

"I didn't do it." He says he didn't did it.
(He was en route to Chicago when the
    murders were committed.)
Is O.J. cleared? Oh me! Oh my!
Not quite an air-tight alibi!

Did he do the gross attack?
Did he eat a gross Big Mac?
Did he kill and then drive back?
Did he bump into the shack?

Kato says he heard a Whoomp!
He saw the Fedders go Caloomp!
A "Whoomp! Caloomp!" can make you queasy.
To find the intruder won't be easy.

A bloody glove.
A glove with blood.
Found near the AC that went "Thud!"
"Aha!" said Fuhrman, Detective, L.A.
I just picked up Exhibit A.

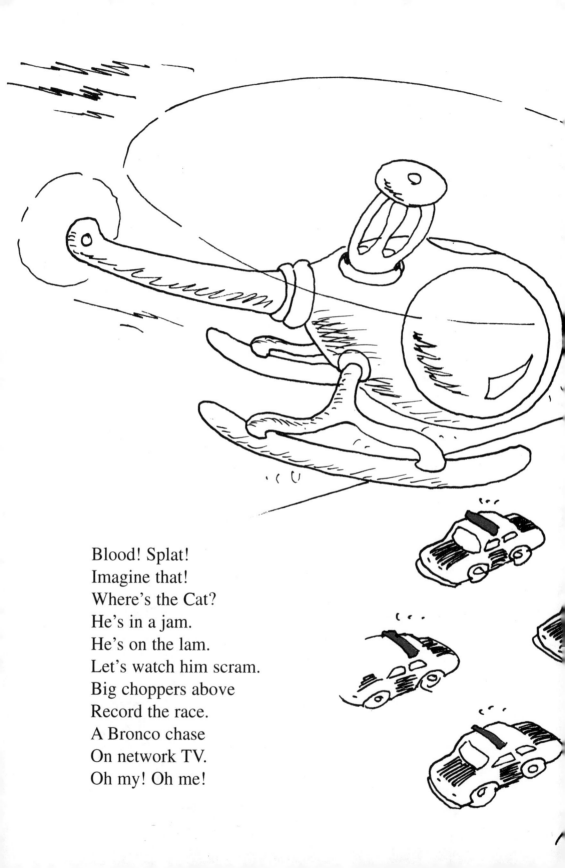

Blood! Splat!
Imagine that!
Where's the Cat?
He's in a jam.
He's on the lam.
Let's watch him scram.
Big choppers above
Record the race.
A Bronco chase
On network TV.
Oh my! Oh me!

"The Juice is loose!"
The sports fans howl.
He's taking off with his pal Al!
A pal named Al can save the day
When you try to get away.

But Juice gave in.
And in a blink
They dipped his all-star hands in ink.
Then snapped his photo, front and side
And said, "Big man, you will be tried!"

One of football's greatest stars
Now sequestered behind bars.
Wearing 32 no more
But "BK401397061794."

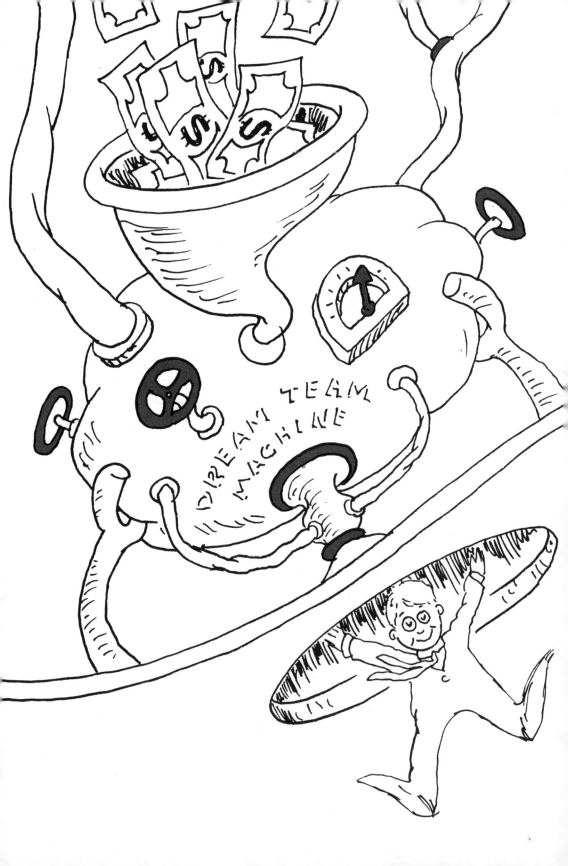

A plea went out to Rob Shapiro
Can you save the fallen hero?
And Marcia Clark, hooray, hooray
Was called in with a justice play.

A man this famous
Never hires
Lawyers like
Jacoby-Meyers.
When you're accused of a killing scheme
You need to build a real Dream Team.

Cochran! Cochran!
Doodle-doo
Johnnie, won't you join the crew?
Cochran! Cochran!
Deedle-dee
The Dream Team needs a victory.

And who will sit upon the bench?
They need a level-headed mensch.
Someone cool-o, smart-o, neat-o.
Let's get good old Judge Lance Ito!

I do not like pre-trial exams.
Green-fisted witnesses, surely shams.
Take an oath, then sell your story
To Geraldo, Phil or Maury.
To anyone who comes to call
With bucks for tales of Orenthal.

Stains on the patio!
The rug has patches!
On O.J.'s socks!
Guess what — it matches!
The DNA is all the same.
The whole thing is a bloody shame.

Injury. Perjury.
His jury. Her jury.
This one says he watched the chase.
This one has a sneaky face.
This one has a can of mace.
That one is a real disgrace.

A jury box.
Twelve folks with sox
Who watch their clocks.
(But can't watch Fox.)
They'll hear the poop,
Then as a group
They will decide.
Go free? Get fried?

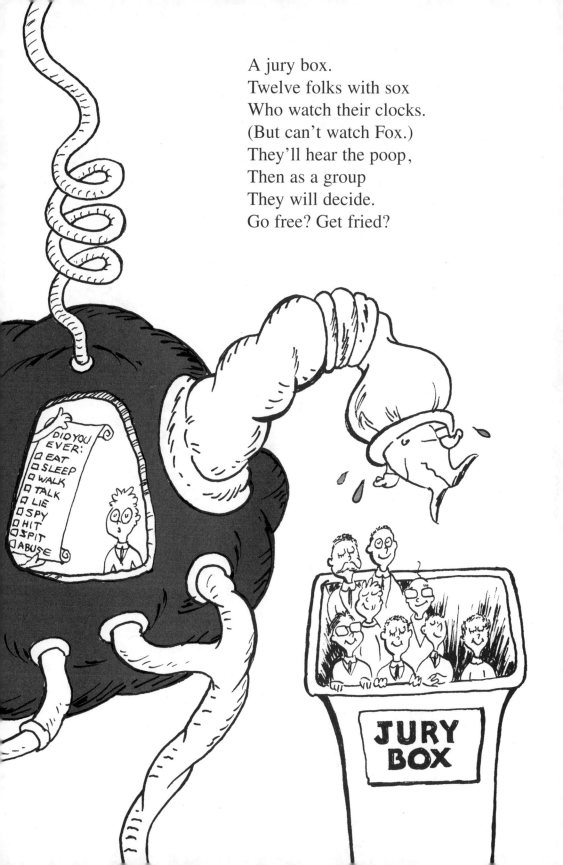

The jury's dropping out like flies.
They bid each other fond goodbyes.

Today at 4, a new exclusive
Tapes that just may prove conclusive.
The jury hears O.J.'s abusive
(Even so, the truth's elusive).

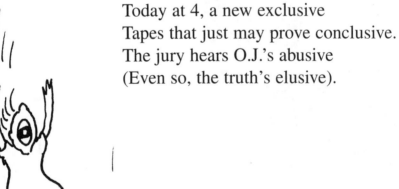

ABC and CBS
Report each angle of this mess.
PBS and NBC
Say "Trial of the Century!"
Will the prosecution botch it?
Who cares? It's on.
So let's all watch it.

A tip from Shipp.
Shipp has a tip.
A slip from O.J.
What a trip!
His words are harsh
His tone extreme.
O.J. had a killing dream!

Says time of death, says Marcia Clark.
When doggy yapped, the bodies found
Quite a trusty bloody hound.

A leather glove.
A dark knit hat.
Allegedly worn by the Cat.
Could this be true?
Could that be fact?
Or is his innocence an act?
Did he strike the fatal blows?
And if he did
Why leave the clothes?

* "There I was, just lickin' my butt, when all of a sudden...such a noise!
I looked at the clock, and made a mental note of the exact time."

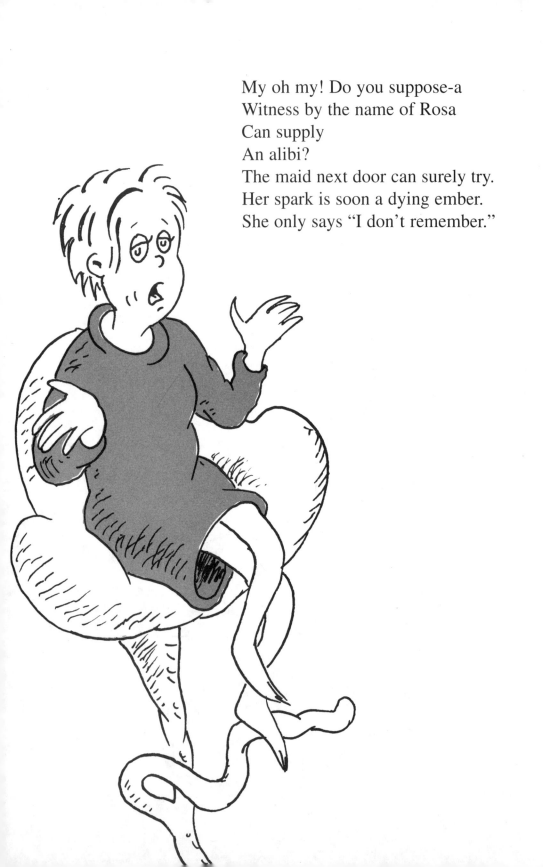

My oh my! Do you suppose-a
Witness by the name of Rosa
Can supply
An alibi?
The maid next door can surely try.
Her spark is soon a dying ember.
She only says "I don't remember."

As F. Lee Bailey takes command
Detective Fuhrman takes the stand.
He found the glove, just lying there.
"Just lying there.
I swear!
I swear!"
A bloody glove, one of a pair.
Evidence is everywhere!

Oh, Kato was eager when he testified.
Though O.J.'s good pal, he couldn't have lied.
He spoke his mind fully.
He said what he meant.
A house guest is faithful
One hundred percent.

When Allan Parks parked
He parked in the dark.
But no one was home
(A real question mark!)
The Bronco was missing!
And so was the Cat.
Until 10:56.
He came out — and that's that!

Blood on the Ford
Could not be ignored.
But the defense complained
'bout how it was stored.
And how 'twas collected
A trainee! Neglected!

A bone-headed play
Which led them astray.
And they had Fung, Fung, Fung
Tell us how they took the samples away.

ITO, ITO,

Our good pal.
We need visits, conjugal.
I miss my friends! I miss my spouse!
I miss my lawn! I miss my house!
This trial's long. This trial's boring.
The testimony's got me snoring.
Give it the ax! Give it the hook!
Just let me go, go write a book!

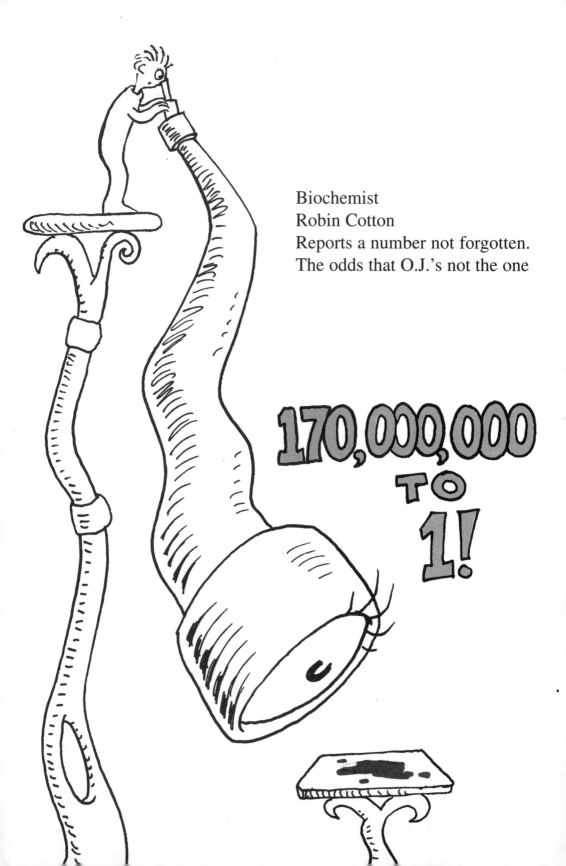

Biochemist
Robin Cotton
Reports a number not forgotten.
The odds that O.J.'s not the one

170,000,000
TO
1!

Fibers! Blood! What evidence!
No wonder the defense was tense!
Then O.J. tried
With all his might
To wear the gloves
But wow — too tight!
The gloves don't fit!
The gloves are snug!
The Cat is thrilled, let's watch him mug!

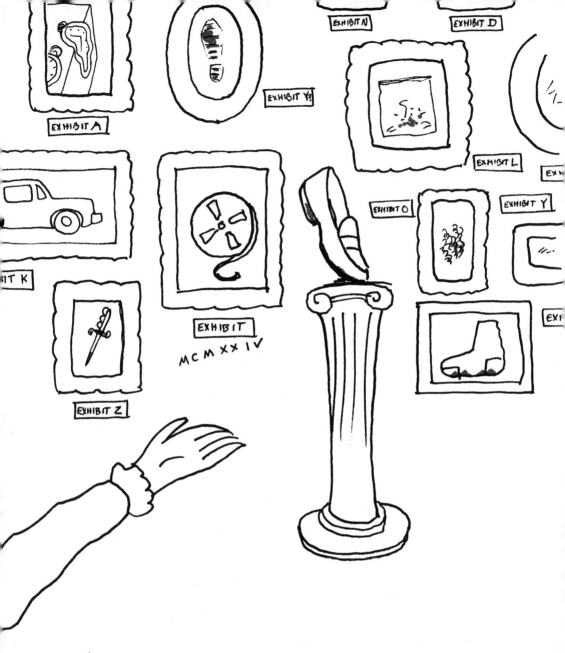

Court TV has followed the ball.
The 57 witnesses fit to call
And hundreds of exhibits that line the wall.
Then Marcia Clark says, "Folks, that's all!"

The defense is up.
The jury's agape
As they watch the Cat joke
  on an exercise tape.
Here's a good move
He tells the fit bunch.
To "accidentally" give
  the wife a punch!

Dream Team! Dream Team!
The experts now stream, seem
To all agree in testimony
That all is evidence is phony.
The glove was planted!
The blood applied!
His innocence can't be denied!

Fuhrman! Fuhrman!
Vicious slur man!
What are we now to infer, man?
It's so hard to trust your word
After the epithets we've heard.

The tapes! The tapes! The tapes are damning!
They're full of nasty racial slamming.
Did Fuhrman plant? Did he connive?
Well all he said's "Amendment Five!"

He does not wish to take the stand.
To put a bible 'neath his hand.
So in that box he will not sit
And don't forget, the gloves don't fit!

The defense rests, then time to close.
So Clark and Darden strike a pose.
You've heard the truth.
You must decree
"The Cat named Juice
be found guilty!"

Then the Dream Team
    makes its pitch
To the jurors
    (who'll soon be rich).
"Remember the gloves?
    They didn't fit
And because that's so,
    you must acquit!"

The jurors leave,
    and now debate.
The verdict
    (how long must we wait?)
It takes an hour,
    then two, then three...
The foreman says,
    "We all agree."

IN BY
10:00
OUT BY
3:00

The weekend passes.
The nation's hushed.
What kind of verdict
Could be that rushed?
On Monday morning
October 2
The jury says, "You're free! Now shoo!
All 12 of us are certain that
The Cat is The Cat Not in the Hat."

Marcia weeps.
The Dream Team cheers.
The nation cries.
It sighs.
It sneers.

That's it.
We're done.
Now all go home.
Go golf. Go dance.
Go sell your tome.

JUICE + ST / JUSTICE

Hmm...take the word JUICE.
Then add ST.
Between the U and I, you see.
And then you have JUSTICE.
Or maybe you don't.
Maybe we will.
And maybe we won't.

'Cause if the Cat didn't do it,
Then who? Then who?
Was it him?
Was it her?
Was it me?
Was it you?
Oh me! Oh my!
Oh my! Oh me!
The murderer is running free…

ALAN KATZ has been a comedy writer and creator for more than 20 years, developing a wide array of projects for television, print and corporate America. He is the author of *Whacked! The Adventures of Tonya Harding and Her Pals* and author of the upcoming *Wackronyms*. His writing credits include *Kids Are People, Too* and Disney's *Raw Toonage,* for which he received an Emmy nomination.

CHRIS WRINN is a top Advertising Illustrator and Art Director in both New York and Connecticut. Her distinctive use of design and color have made major contributions to well-known advertising campaigns. Her first love is fine art. Her work is on permanent display at the Soundview Gallery in Long Island, New York, as well as at other notable galleries from New England to Florida. She has also completed a body of work that hangs in private collections.

ISBN 0-7871-0956-8
Printed in the United States of America

DOVE BOOKS
301 North Cañon Drive • Beverly Hills, CA 90210
Distributed by Penguin USA

Text and cover layout by Rick Penn-Kraus

First Printing: March 1996
10 9 8 7 6 5 4 3 2 1